T0058133

Ulysses Press

TM & © 2019 Wiz Khalifa under license from Atlantic Recording Corporation.
All rights reserved. www.wizkhalifa.com.
Design copyright © 2019 Ulysses Press and its licensors. All rights reserved. Any unauthorized duplication in whole or in part or dissemination of this edition by any means (including but not limited to photocopying, electronic devices, digital versions, and the internet) will be prosecuted to the fullest extent of the law.

Published in the United States by:
Ulysses Press
P.O. Box 3440
Berkeley, CA 94703
www.ulyssespress.com

ISBN: 978-1-61243-895-5

Printed in Canada by Marquis Book Printing

2 4 6 8 10 9 7 5 3 1

Illustrations © Metamoki LLC

Distributed by Publishers Group West

Y'ALL READY TO BLAZE AND COLOR IN THIS KUSH?

HOLLYWOOD
LOS ANGELES

TAYLOR
GANG

Dog
DOG
FOOD

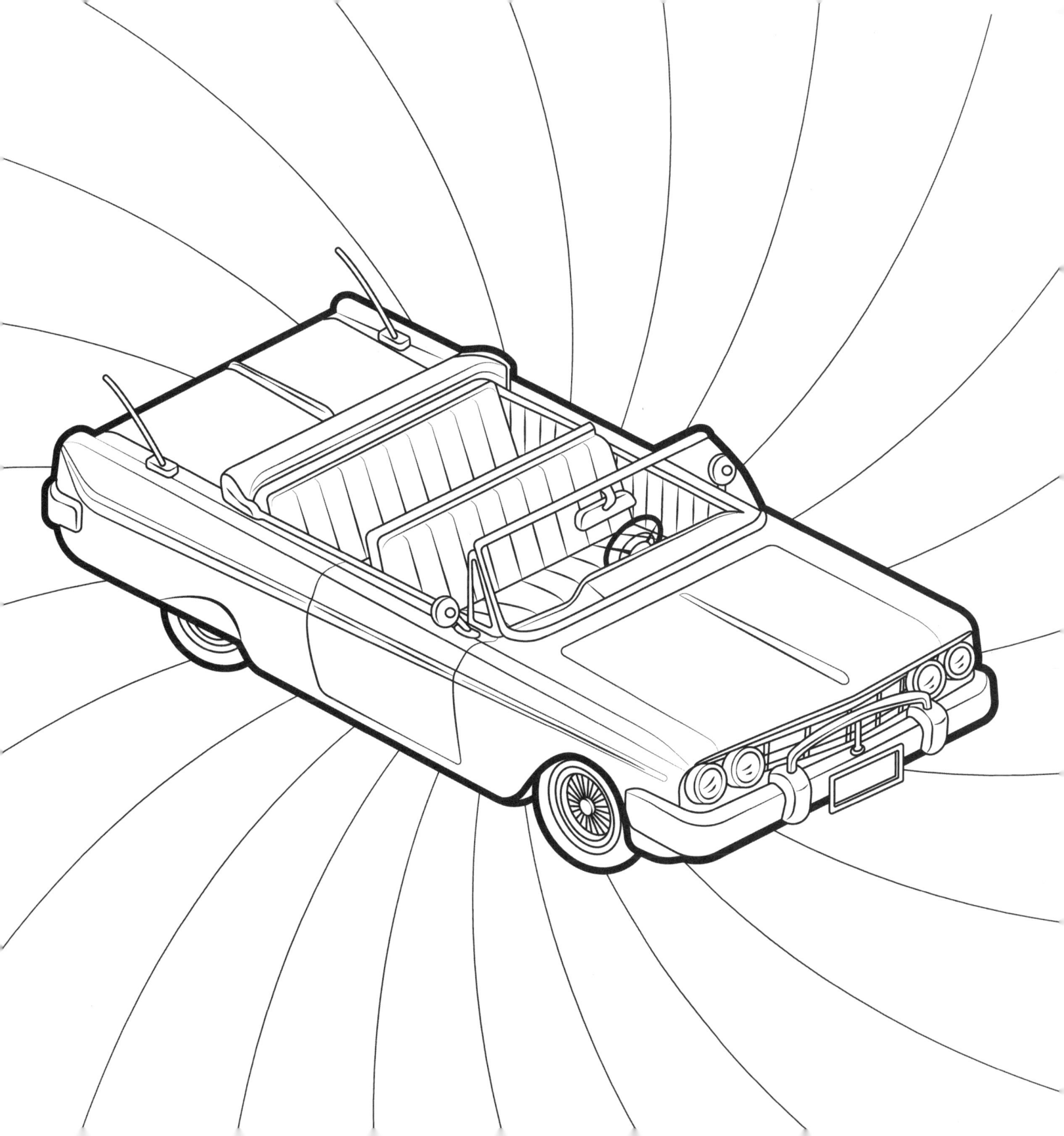

Ck
Kk

Gdp
Cd

VALENTINE'S DAY

Pu
Kk

Jv
Jv
My Valentine
Ag

CABO

Kk
A9

Cd
Jh

$1
$1

4TH OF JULY

Kk
Pu
Pu

Jh
Jh
Ck

PARIS

6666

Ag
Kk

Cd
Jh
Jh
Cannabis
Bread

WIZ'S BIRTHDAY

Kk
Happy Birthday
Ag

Cd
Ck

AMSTERDAM

Amsterdam
STAR

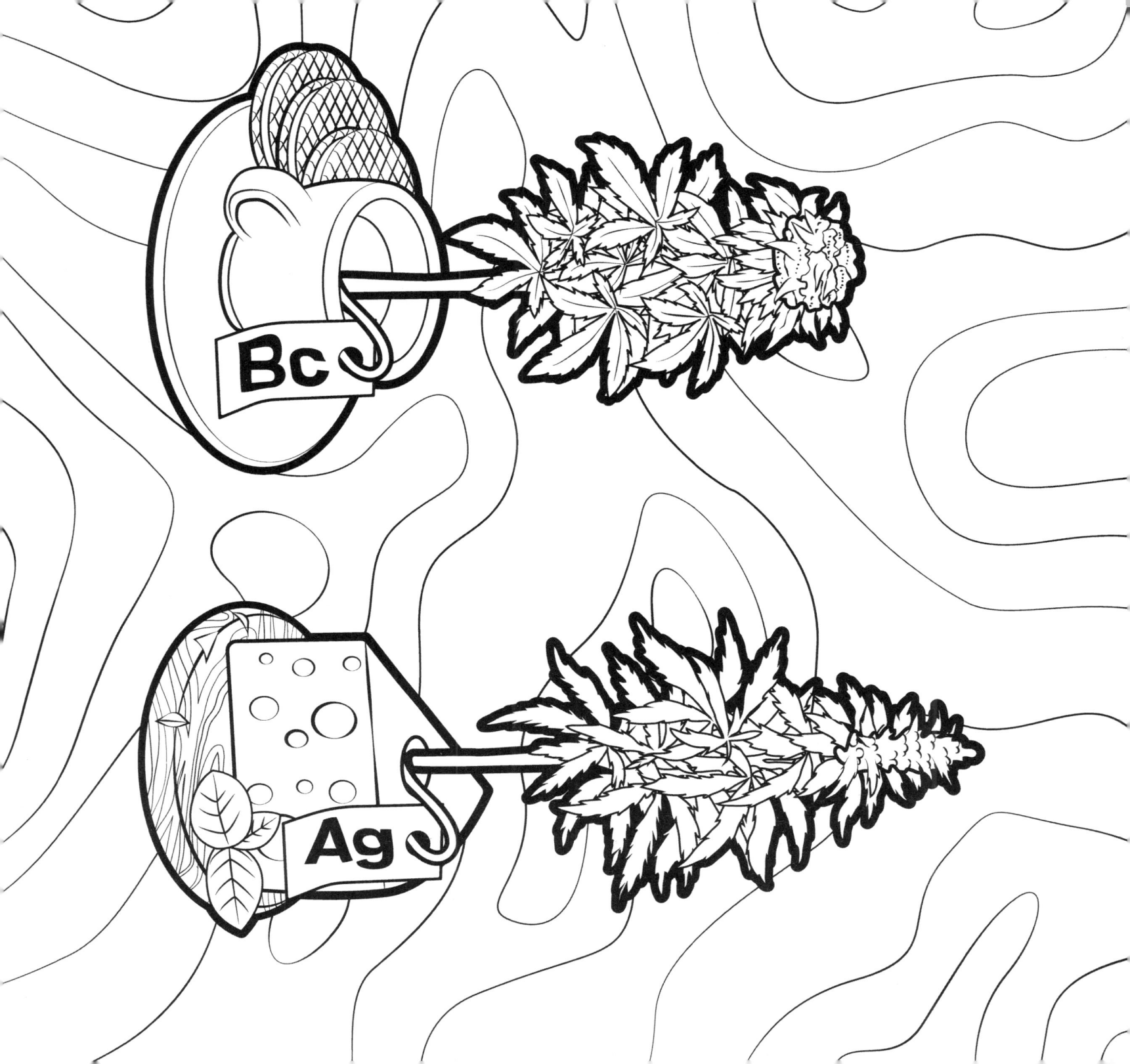
Bc
Ag

Cd
Jh
Jh

HALLOWEED

Kkd
Vm

I.P.
Tp
Tp
WZ

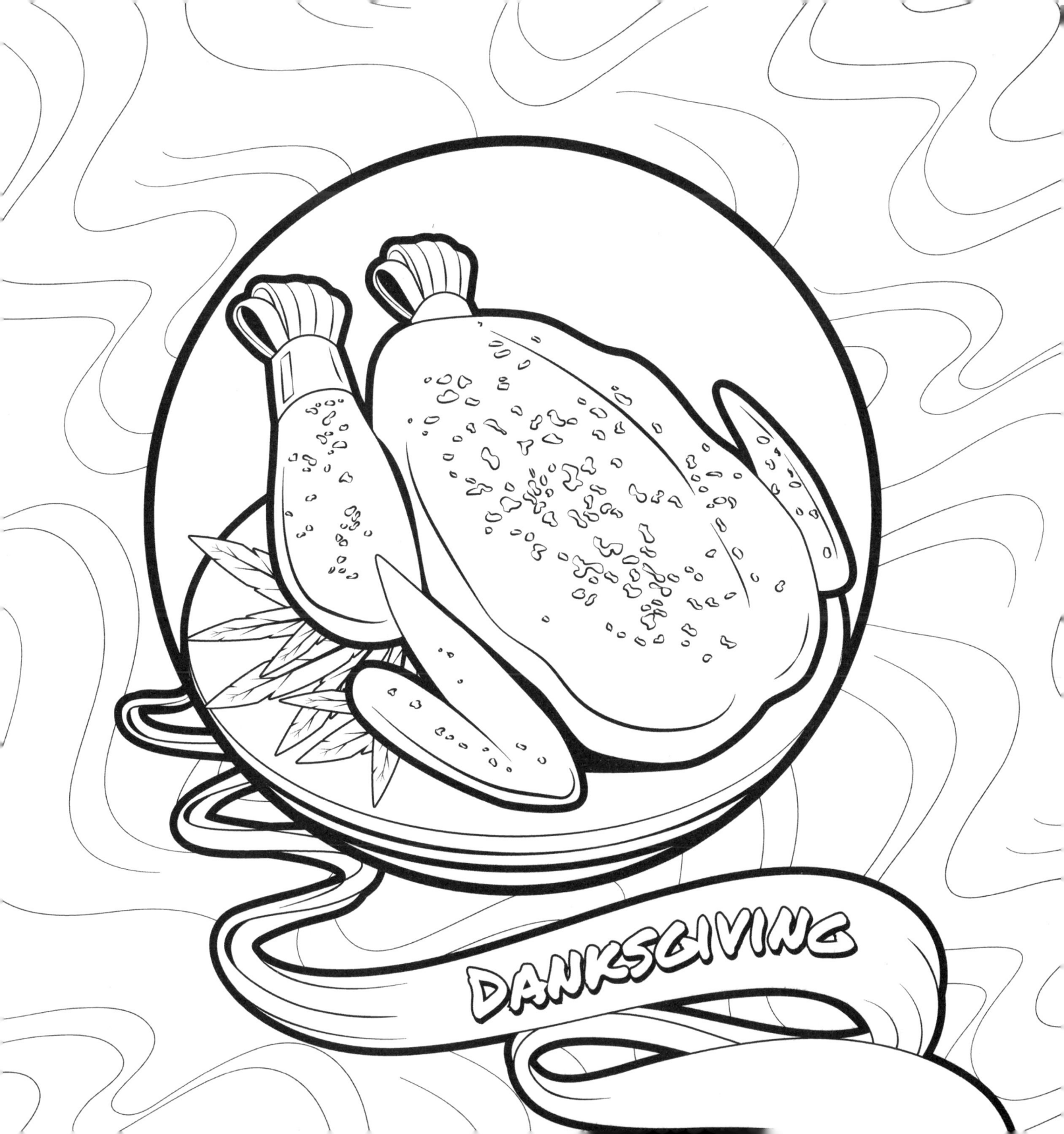
DANKSGIVING

Jh
Jh
Ck

Ag
Ck

TORONTO

Kg
Wnl

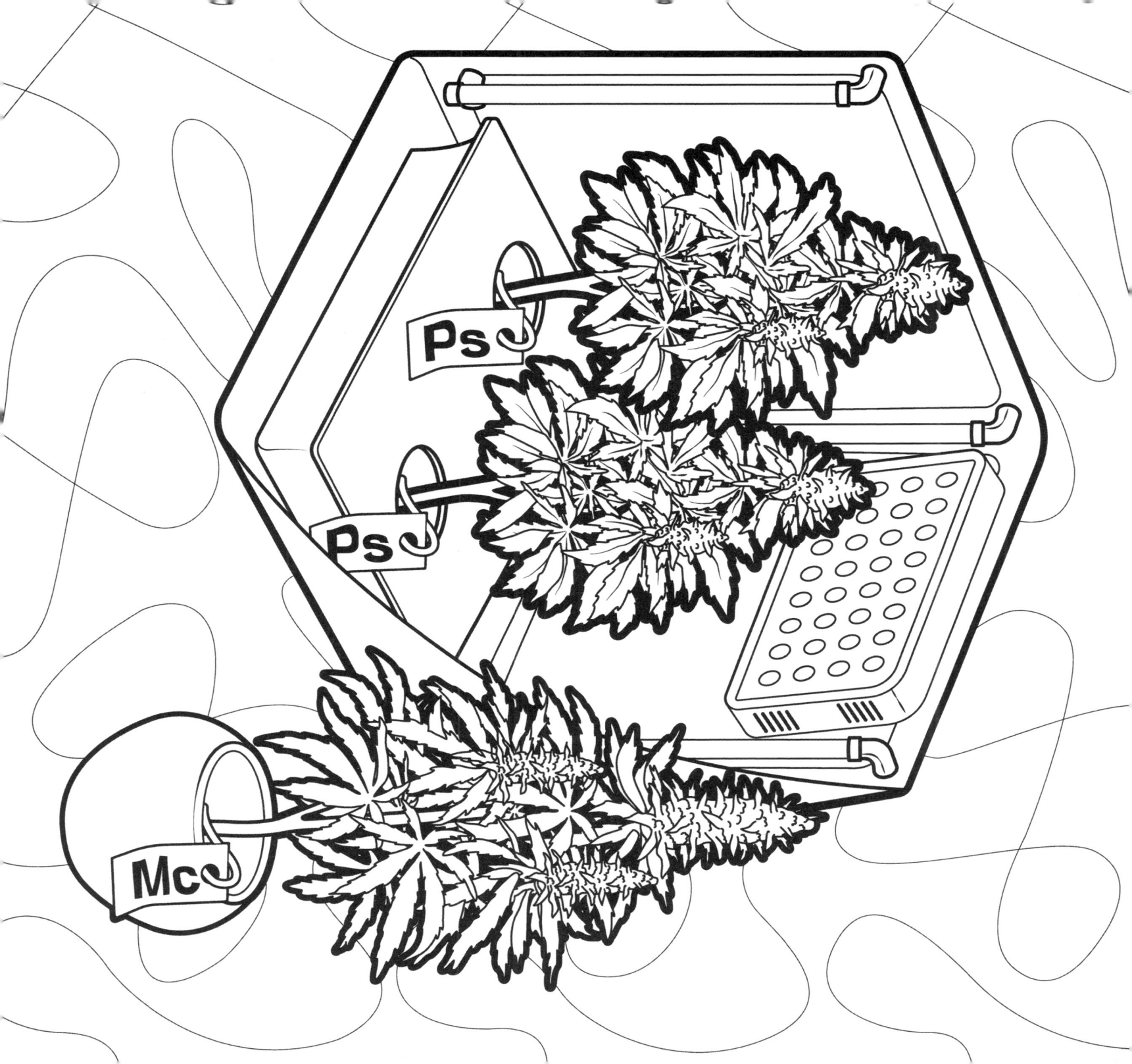
Ps
Ps
Mc

MERRY KUSHMAS

Bc
Bc
Kk

Cd
Jh

LAS VEGAS

CAM

Kkv
Gdv

BLACK JACK
Jv
Jv
Vk